Chord by Chord
Greatest Hits
Arranged by Kenneth Baker

Are You Lonesome Tonight **20**
Banks Of The Ohio **4**
Bye Bye Love **6**
Candle In The Wind **16**
Drifting And Dreaming **11**
He'll Have To Go **28**
I Can See Clearly Now **32**
If I Ever Lose My Faith In You **30**
Love Is Blue **34**
O Sole Mio **8**
Portrait Of My Love **22**
She Wears My Ring **18**
Sometimes When We Touch **12**
Tennessee Waltz **14**
Theme From Pastoral Symphony **5**
Ticket To Ride **38**
Unchained Melody **26**
Where Have All The Flowers Gone **10**
Words **24**
World **36**

This book © Copyright 1999 Chester Music
Order No. CH61380 ISBN 0-7119-6562-5

Chester Music
(A division of Music Sales Limited)
8/9 Frith Street
London W1V 5TZ

Introduction

What's special about this book?

- In this book you will **improve your playing in easy stages,** simply through playing great pieces... from **Are You Lonesome Tonight** and **Candle In The Wind** to **Unchained Melody**.

- The common problem of a 'lazy left hand' technique is solved by the unique **chord-by-chord symbols** (explained opposite).

What standard do I need to be?

- To start this book you should be working at, or have already worked through **Chord By Chord Book 1**, or be the equivalent of Grade 1 Associated Board standard.

What will I learn?

- In this book you continue your study of simple left hand **triads** in various forms and with different rhythmic variations.

- **Easy explanations** of the different technical points are included at every stage. As always, you will be able to play lots of **well-known pop songs!**

How will the CD help?

- The CD allows you to **hear** how every song should be played and to **play along with a full backing band.** You will find these audio facilities an enormous advantage when learning to play the piano from these books.

How to use the CD...

- On the CD there are a number of lead-in 'clicks' (cymbal beats) at the beginning of every track in order to set the speed. There are four clicks with 4/4 time, three clicks with 3/4 time and so on.

- On many of the tracks these lead-in clicks are followed by a short musical 'introduction' from the backing band. You start playing when you hear the solo piano on the backing track begin.

The **chord by chord** symbols in this book indicate a **triad**.
This is a three note chord with the following spacing:

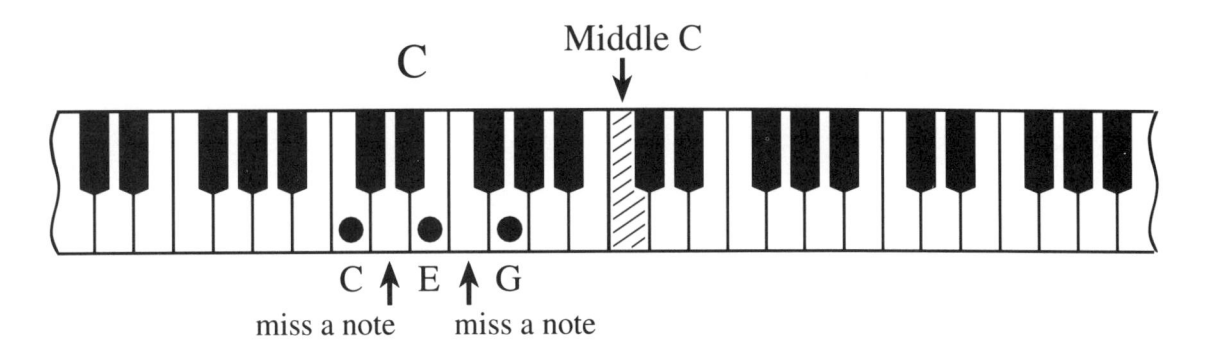

C ↑ E ↑ G
miss a note   miss a note

A triad takes its name from its **bottom note**,
so the above chord is called C.

Here are F and G triads:

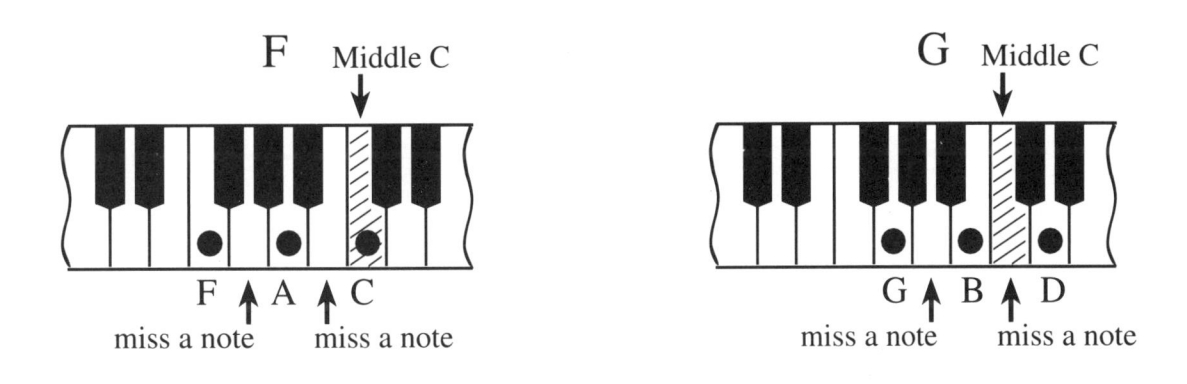

F ↑ A ↑ C
miss a note   miss a note

G ↑ B ↑ D
miss a note   miss a note

On the piano, triads can be used to create simple but effective left hand accompaniments. The fingering is always the same:

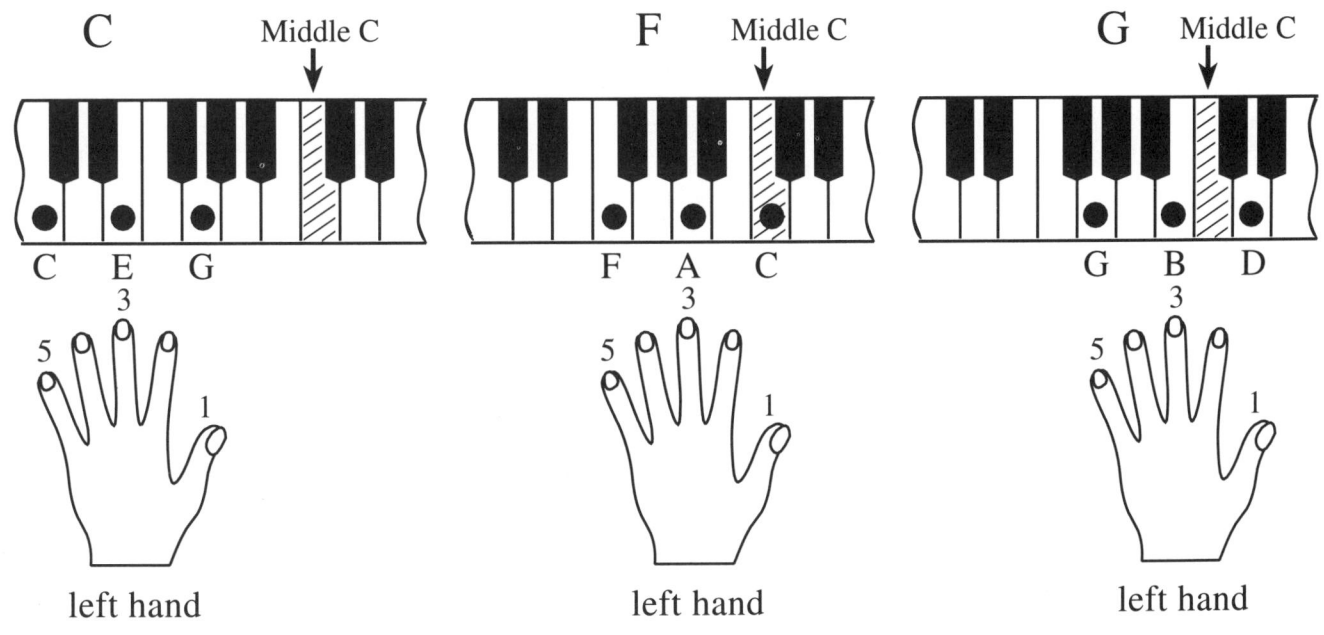

C E G
5 3 1
left hand

F A C
5 3 1
left hand

G B D
5 3 1
left hand

In the **chord by chord** symbols, **middle C** is indicated by a shaded note.

Banks Of The Ohio

Traditional

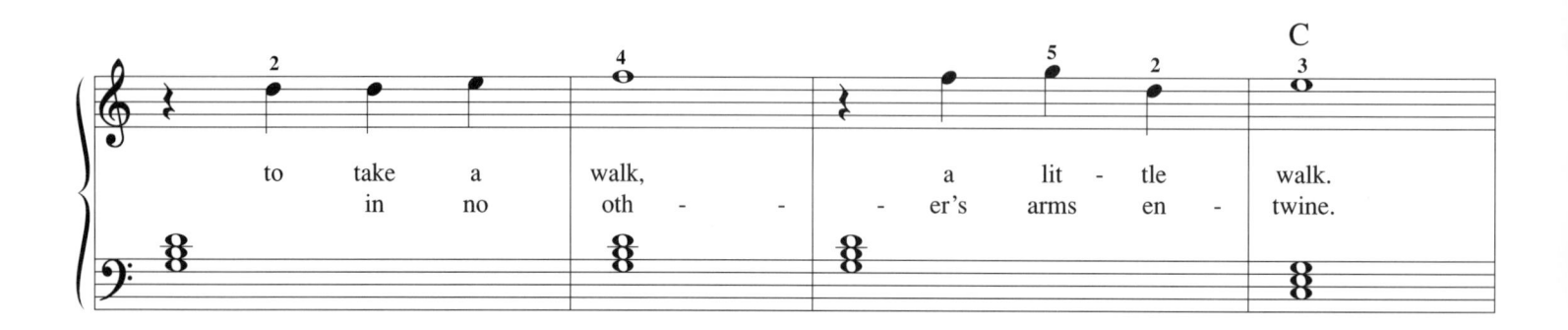

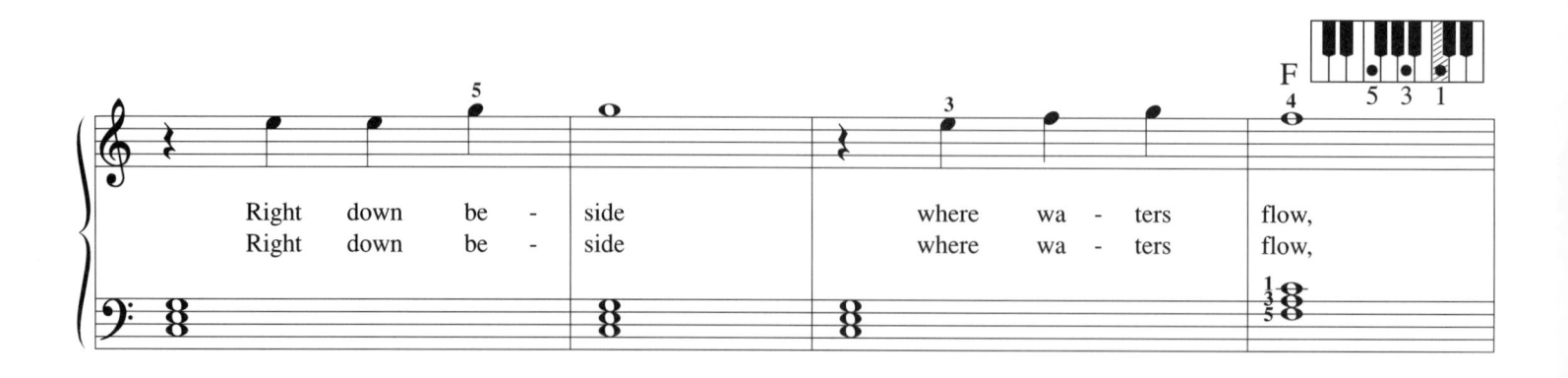

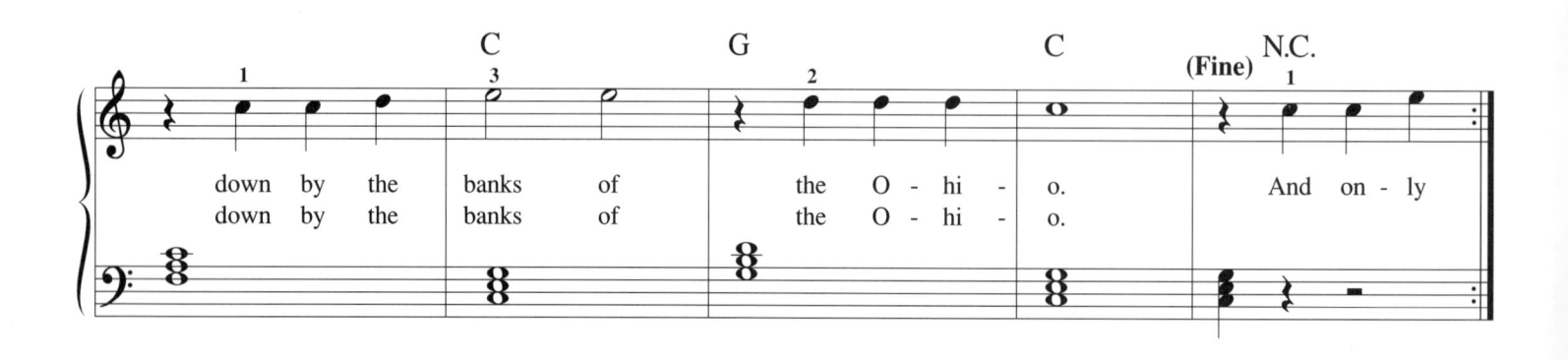

♩ = 128

I asked my love to take a walk, to take a walk, a little walk.
Right down be-side where wa-ters flow, down by the banks of the O-hi-o. And on-ly

say that you'll be mine, in no oth-er's arms en-twine.
Right down be-side where wa-ters flow, down by the banks of the O-hi-o.

© Copyright 1999 Dorsey Brothers Music Limited, 8/9 Frith Street, London W1.
All Rights Reserved. International Copyright Secured.

Theme From The Pastoral Symphony

By Ludwig van Beethoven

Bye Bye Love

Words & Music by Felice & Boudleaux Bryant

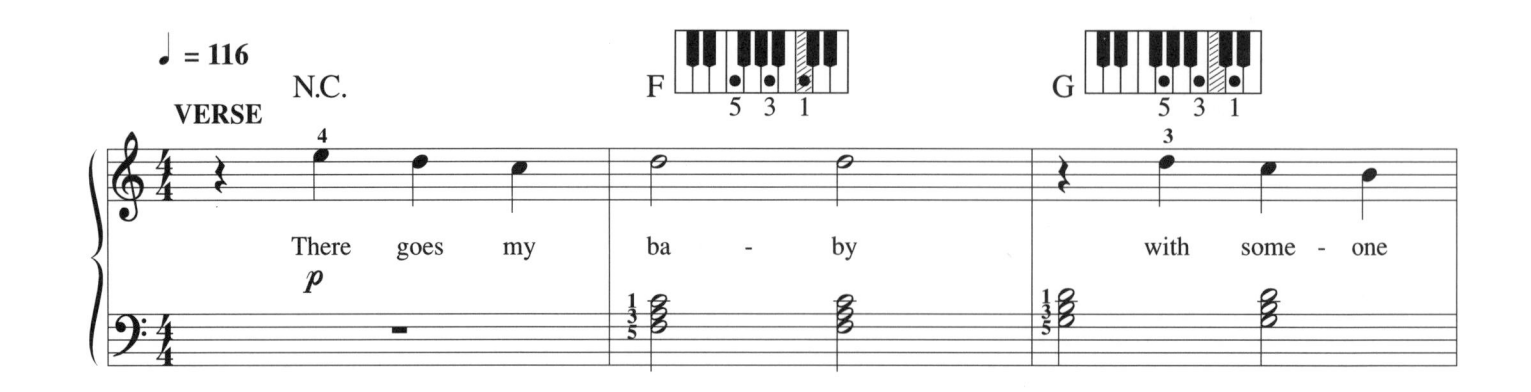

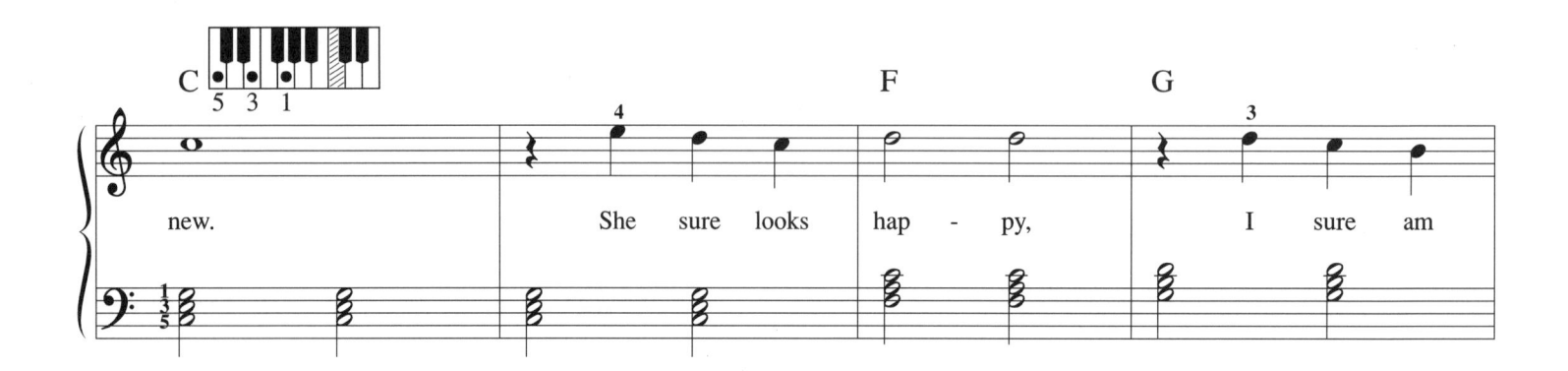

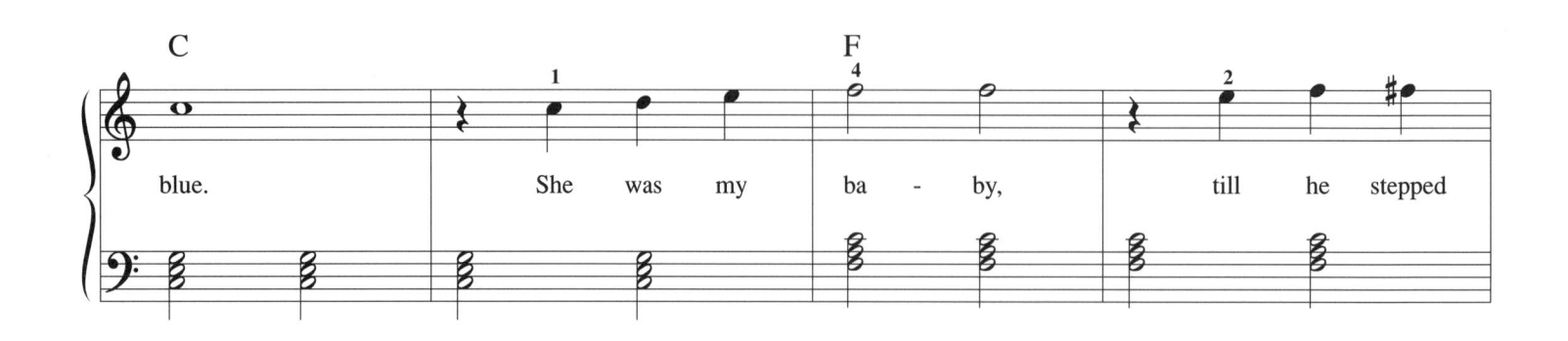

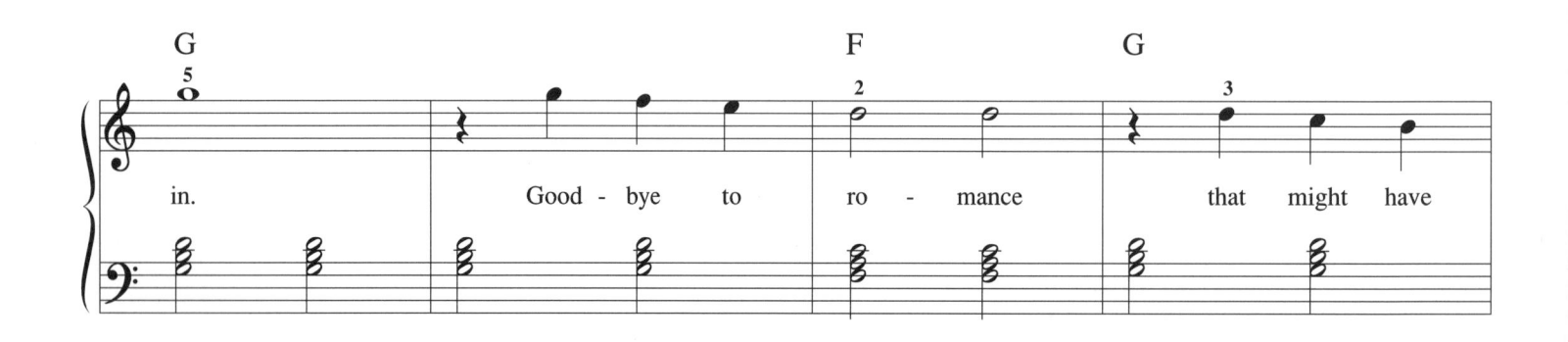

♩ = 116

VERSE

There goes my baby with someone new. She sure looks happy, I sure am blue. She was my baby, till he stepped in. Goodbye to romance that might have

© Copyright 1957 House Of Bryant Publications, USA.
Acuff-Rose Music Limited, 25 James Street, London W1.
All Rights Reserved. International Copyright Secured.

CHORUS

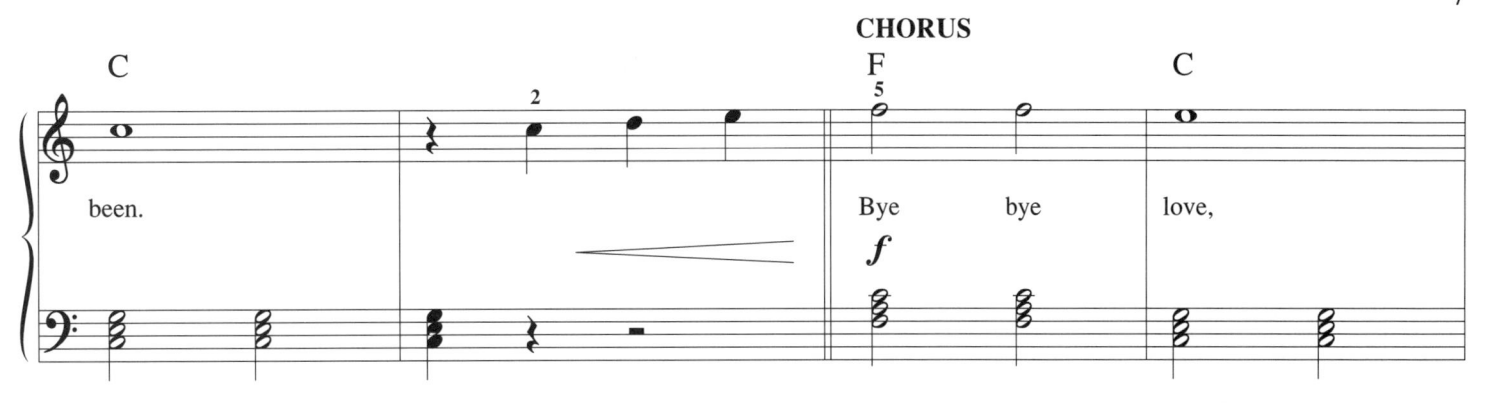

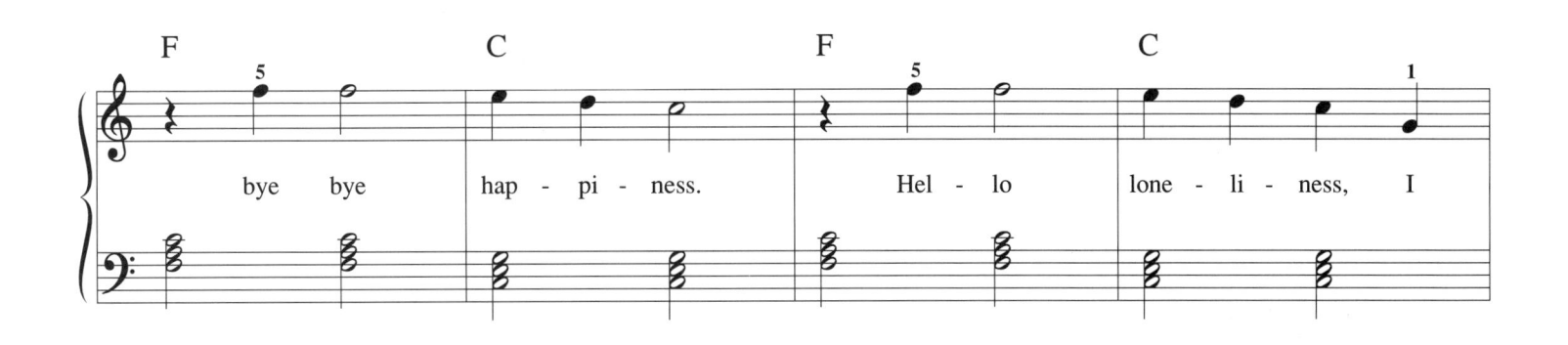

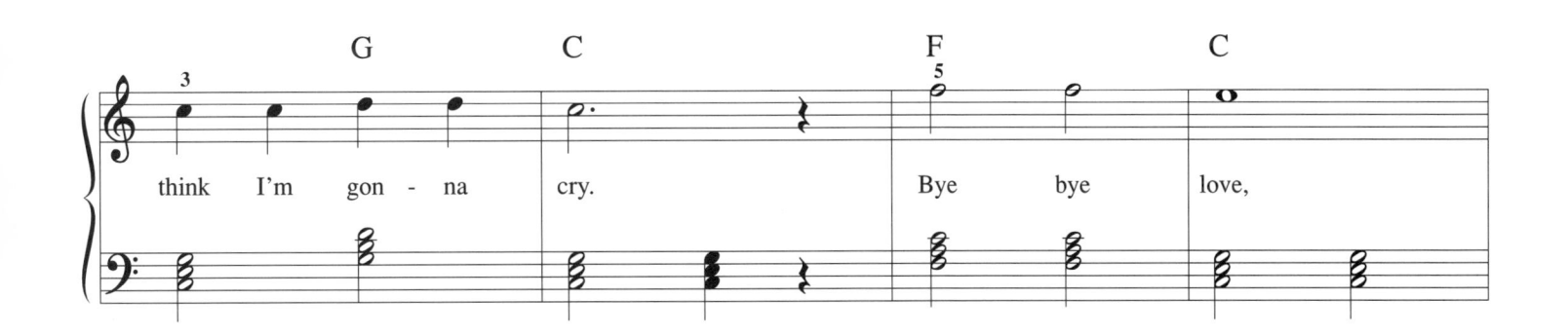

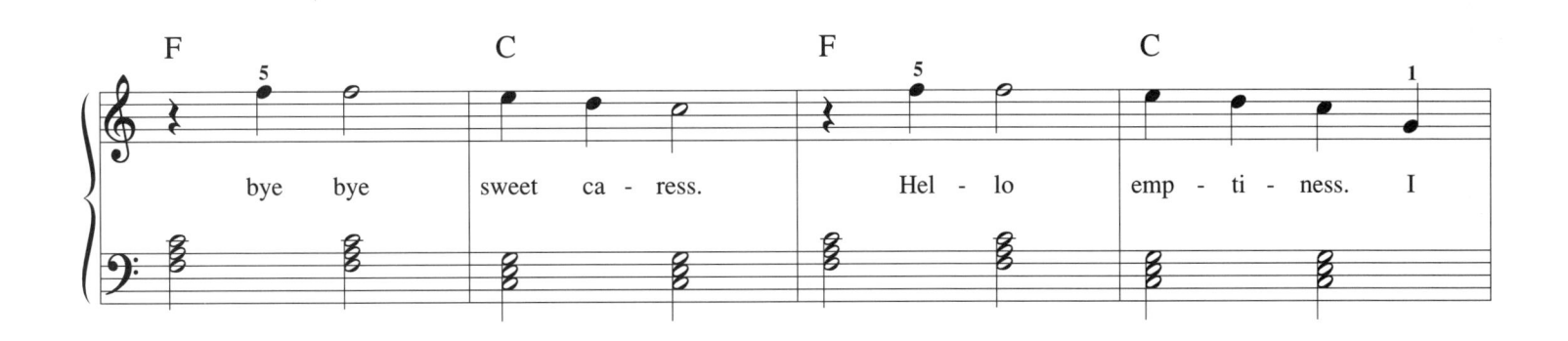

been. Bye bye love, bye bye happiness. Hello loneliness, I think I'm gonna cry. Bye bye love, bye bye sweet caress. Hello emptiness. I feel like I could die. Bye bye, my love, bye bye.

O Sole Mio

Music by Edorado di Capua. Words by Giovanni Capurro

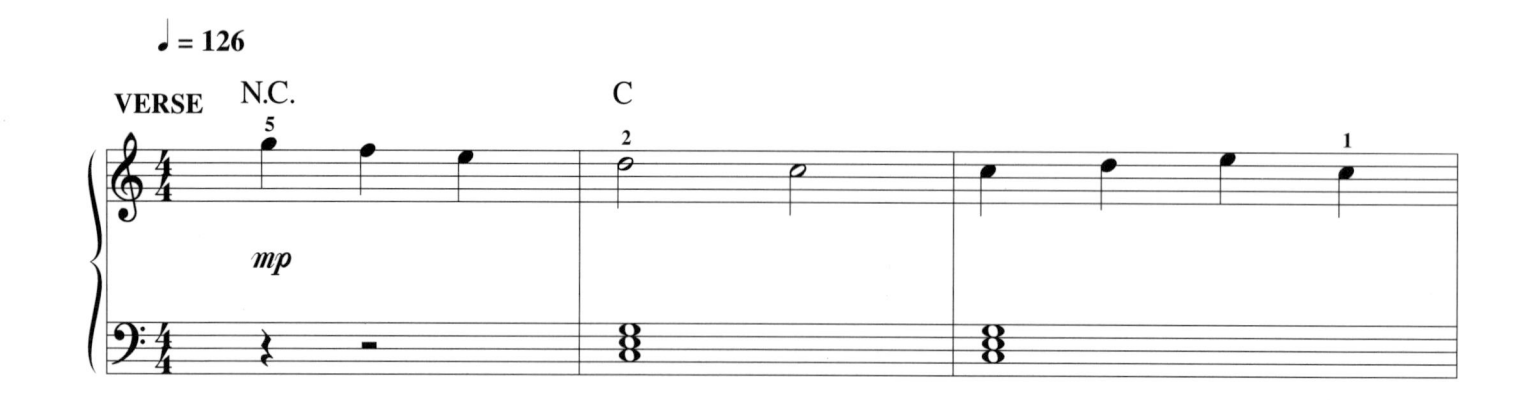

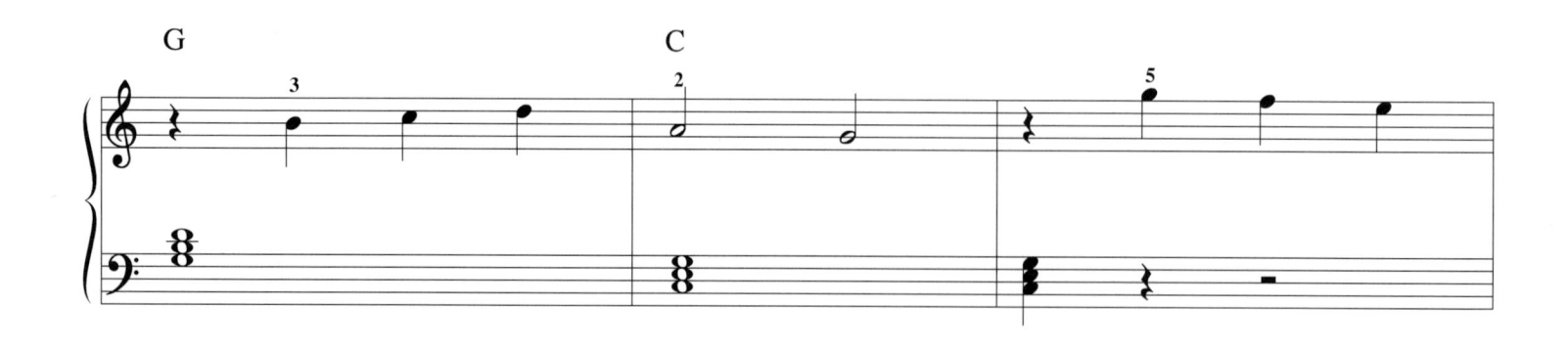

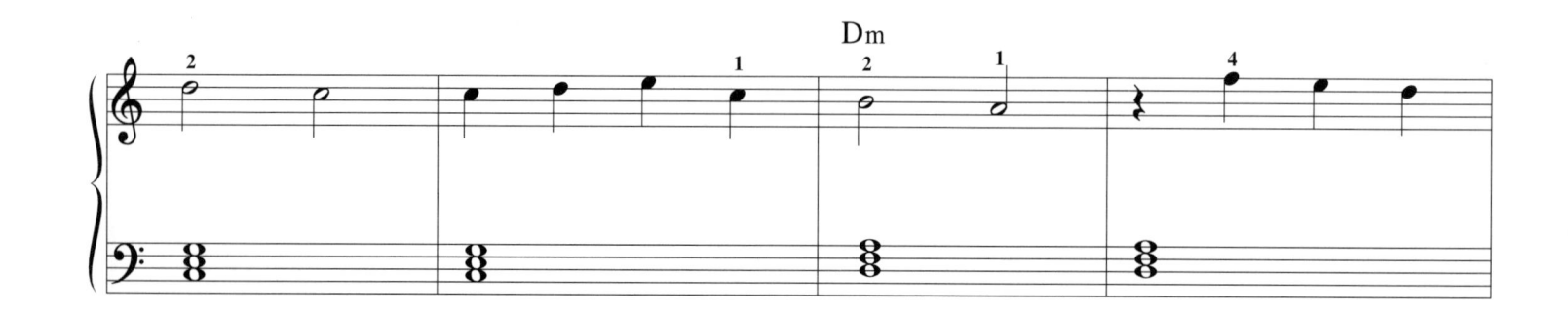

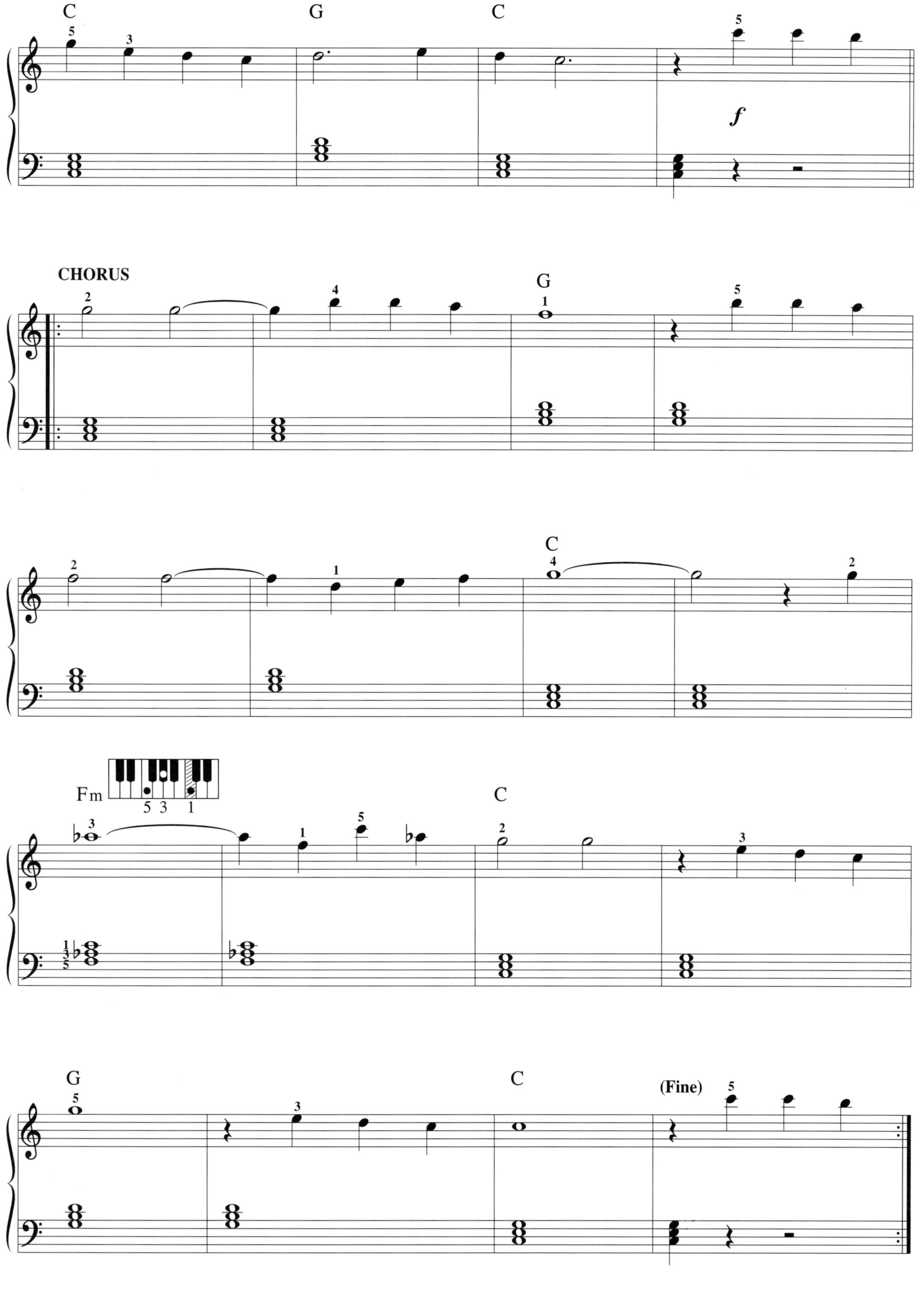
C
G
C
f
CHORUS
G
C
Fm
5 3 1
C
G
C
(Fine)

Where Have All The Flowers Gone

Words & Music by Pete Seeger

Drifting And Dreaming (Sweet Paradise)

Words by Haven Gillespie. Music by Egbert Van Alstyne,
Erwin R. Schmidt & Loyal Curtis

Drift-ing and dream-ing, while sha-dows fall.

Soft-ly at twi-light, I hear you call.

Love's old sweet sto-ry, told with your eyes.

Drift-ing and dream-ing, sweet pa-ra-dise.

© Copyright 1925 Edwin H. Morris & Company Incorporated, USA.
Copyright renewed and assigned to Edwin H. Morris & Company Incorporated.
Campbell Connelly & Company Limited, 8/9 Frith Street, London W1 (83.33%)/
Redwood Music Limited, Iron Bridge House, 3 Bridge Approach, London NW1 (16.67%).
All Rights Reserved. International Copyright Secured.

Sometimes When We Touch

Words & Music by Dan Hill & Barry Mann

♩ = 100

VERSE

You ask me if I love you, and I choke on my reply. I'd rather hurt you honestly, than mislead you with a lie. And who am I to judge you on what you say or do? I'm

© Copyright 1977 McCauley Music, Mann and Weill Songs Incorporated &
ATV Music Corporation for the World. © Copyright 1977 ATV Music, London WC2.
All Rights Reserved. International Copyright Secured.

13

only just be-ginning to see the real you. And

CHORUS

some-times when we touch, the ho-nes-ty's too much, and I

have to close my eyes and hide. I wan-na

hold you till I die, till we both break down and cry, I wan-na

hold you till the fear in me sub-sides.

Tennessee Waltz

Words & Music by Redd Stewart & Pee Wee King

I was waltzing with my darlin' to the Tennessee Waltz, when an old friend I happened to see. Introduced him to my loved one, and while they were waltzing, my

* this Am chord is played one octave (eight notes) lower than usual, for convenience.

© Copyright 1948 Acuff-Rose Music Incorporated, USA.
Cinephonic Music Company Limited, 8/9 Frith Street, London W1.
All Rights Reserved. International Copyright Secured.

friend stole my sweet-heart from me. I re-member the night, and the Ten-nes-see Waltz. Now I know just how much I have lost. Yes, I lost my lit-tle dar-lin', the night they were play-ing the beau-ti-ful Ten-nes-see Waltz.

Candle In The Wind

Words & Music by Elton John & Bernie Taupin

♩ = 120

VERSE

Good-bye Nor-ma Jean, though I ne-ver knew you at all, you had the grace to hold your-self while those a-round you crawled. They crawled out of the wood-work, and they whis-pered in-to your brain, they set you on a

© Copyright 1973 for the world by Dick James Music Limited, 47 British Grove, London W4.
All Rights Reserved. International Copyright Secured.

tread-mill, and they made you change your name. And it

CHORUS

seems to me you lived your life like a can-dle in the wind, ne-ver

mf

know-ing who to cling to when the rain set in. And I

would have liked to have known you, but I was just a kid, your can-dle had burned out

long be-fore your le-gend ev-er did.

p

She Wears My Ring

Words & Music by Felice & Boudleaux Bryant

love for all the world to see. This tiny ring is a to-ken of ten-der e-mo-tion, an end-less pool of love, that's as deep as the o - - cean. She swears to wear it with e-ter-nal de-vo-tion, that's why I sing, be-cause she wears my ring.

Are You Lonesome Tonight

Words & Music by Roy Turk & Lou Handman

*this "A" chord is played one octave (eight notes) lower than usual, for convenience.

© Copyright 1926 Bourne Company, USA.
Redwood Music Limited, Iron Bridge House, 3 Bridge Approach, London NW1 for the
Commonwealth of Nations, Eire, Germany, Austria, Switzerland, South Africa & Spain.
All Rights Reserved. International Copyright Secured.

kissed you and called you "Sweet-heart?" _____ Do the
chairs in your par-lour seem emp-ty and bare, do you
gaze at the door-step, and pic-ture me there? Is your
heart filled with pain, shall I come back a-gain? Tell me,
dear, are you lone-some to-night? _____

Portrait Of My Love

Words by David West. Music by Cyril Ornadel

Lyrics:

There could ne-ver be a por-trait of my love,
for no-bo-dy could paint a dream.
You will ne-ver see a por-trait of my love,
for mi-ra-cles are ne-ver seen.

A - - - ny-one who

sees her, soon forgets the Mona Lisa. It would take, I know a Michelange- lo, and he would need the glow of dawn that paints the sky above, to try and paint a portrait of my love.

Words

Words & Music by Barry Gibb, Robin Gibb & Maurice Gibb

now there'll be no oth-er time, and I can show you how, my love.

Talk is e-ver-last-ing words, and de-di-cate them all to me, and

I will give you all my life, I'm here if you should call to me. You

think that I don't e-ven mean a sin-gle word I say, it's on-ly

words, and words are all I have to take your heart a-way.

Unchained Melody

Words by Hy Zaret. Music by Alex North

♩ = 120

CHORUS

Oh, my love, my dar - ling, I've hun - gered for your touch a long, lone - ly time. Time goes by so slow - ly, and time can do so much, are you still

Em G C Dm
mine? I need your love, I
mf
Ped. Ped. Ped. Ped.
Em F G
need your love, God speed your love to
Ped. Ped. Ped. Ped.
INTERLUDE
C (Fine) F G
me.
Lonely rivers flow to the sea,
Lonely rivers sigh, "Wait for
p
Ped. Ped. Ped.
F E♭ F G
to the sea. To the open arms of the
me, wait for me!" I'll be coming home, wait for
Ped. Ped. Ped. Ped.
1. C Em 2. C
D.C. al Fine
sea. me.
Ped. Ped. Ped.

He'll Have To Go

Words & Music by Joe Allison & Audrey Allison

Put your sweet lips a little closer to the 'phone, let's pretend that we're together, all alone. I'll tell the man to turn the jukebox way down low, and you can tell your friend there with you, he'll have to go. You can't say the words I want to hear while you're with a-noth-er man. If you want me, an-swer "yes" or "no", dar-ling, I will un-der-stand. Put your

If I Ever Lose My Faith In You

Words & Music by Sting

♩ = 100

VERSES

1. You could say I lost my faith in Science and progress.
2. Some would say I was a lost man in a lost world.

You could say I lost belief in the Holy Church.
You could say I lost my faith in the people on T.V.

You could say I lost my sense of direction.
You could say I lost my belief in our politicians.

Yes, you could say all of this and worse, but
They all seem like game show hosts to me, but

© Copyright 1993 G.M. Sumner & Steerpike Limited.
EMI Music Publishing Limited/Magnetic Publishing Limited.
All Rights Reserved. International Copyright Secured.

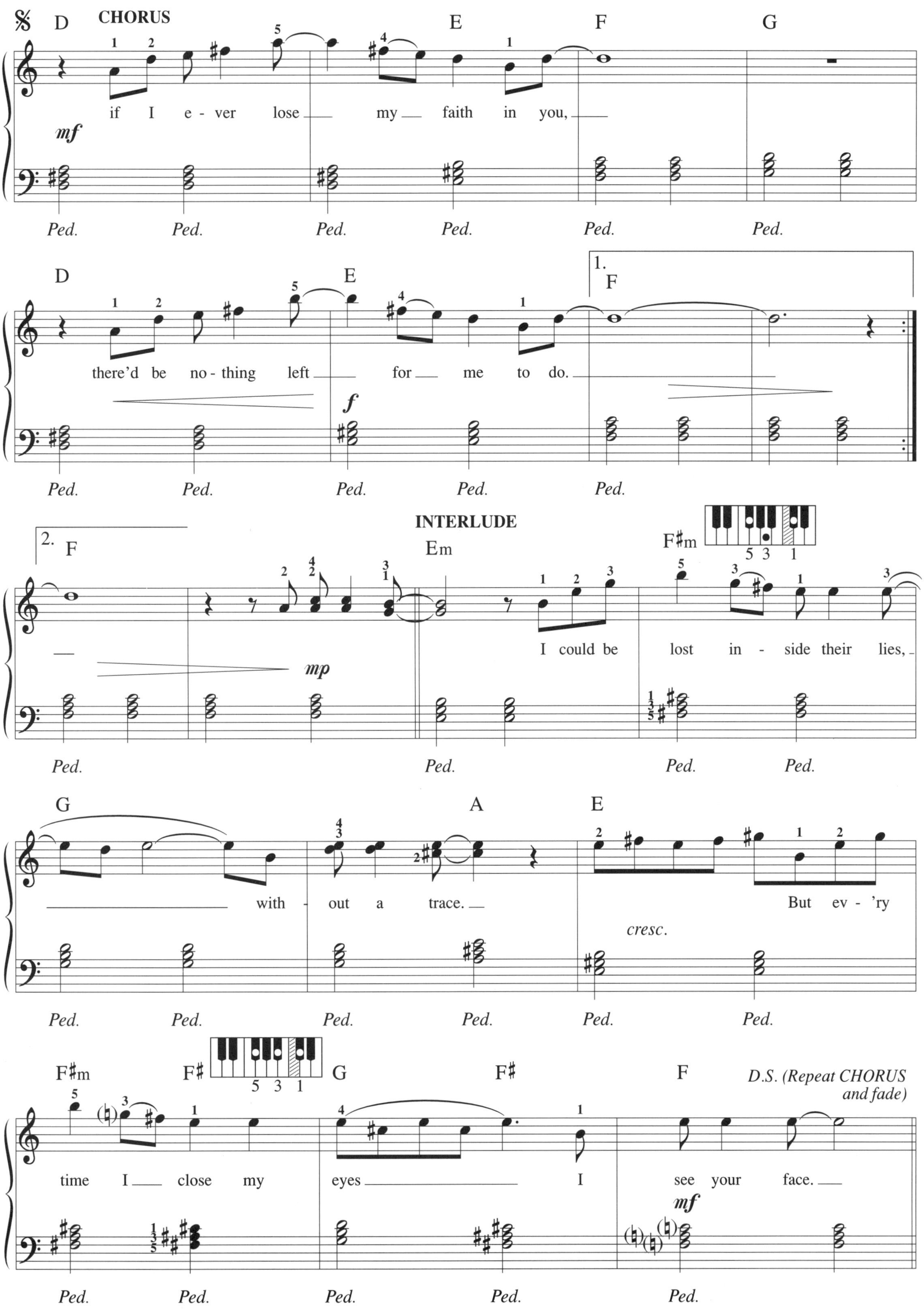
CHORUS
D E F G
if I e - ver lose my faith in you,
mf
Ped. Ped. Ped. Ped. Ped. Ped.
D E
1. F
there'd be no - thing left for me to do.
f
Ped. Ped. Ped. Ped. Ped.
2. F
INTERLUDE
Em
F♯m
5 3 1
I could be lost in - side their lies,
mp
Ped. Ped. Ped. Ped.
G A E
with - out a trace.
But ev - 'ry
cresc.
Ped. Ped. Ped. Ped. Ped. Ped.
F♯m F♯
5 3 1
G F♯ F
D.S. (Repeat CHORUS and fade)
time I close my eyes I see your face.
mf
Ped. Ped. Ped. Ped. Ped.

I Can See Clearly Now

Words & Music by Johnny Nash

♩ = 116
CHORUS
C F C
1.3. I can see clear - ly now, the rain has gone.
2. Think I can make it now, the pain has gone.
mf
Ped.
F
I can see all ob - sta - cles
All of the bad feel - ings have
mp
mf
G C
in my way.
dis - ap - peared.
Gone are the dark
Here is the rain -
F C
clouds that had me blind, it's gon - na be a
- bow I've been pray - ing for, it's gon - na be a
p

© Copyright 1972 by Dovan Music Incorporated, Vanas Music Incorporated & Arnas Music, USA.
Warner Chappell Music Limited, Griffin House, 161 Hammersmith Road, London W6.
All Rights Reserved. International Copyright Secured.

B♭
F
C
bright, bright sun - shi - ny day.
bright, bright sun - shi - ny day.
Ped.
1.
B♭
F
It's gon - na be a bright, bright, sun - shi - ny day.
f
C
(Fine)
2.
INTERLUDE
E♭
Look all a - round there's no - thing but blue skies.
mp
B♭
E♭
Look straight a - head, no - thing but blue skies.
G
F
G
D.C. al Fine
f

Love Is Blue (L'Amour Est Bleu)

Music by Andre Popp. Original Words by Pierre Cour.
English Lyric by Bryan Blackburn

Lyrics:

Blue, blue, my world is blue. Blue is my world, now I'm with-out you. Grey, grey, my life is grey. Cold is my heart, since you went a-way. Red, red, my Black, black, the

* this "A" chord is played one octave (eight notes) lower than usual, for convenience.

© Copyright 1966 Ste.Nouvelles Des Editions Musicales, Paris, France.
Chrysalis Songs Limited, Bramley Road, London W10 (50%)/SDRM (50%).
All Rights Reserved. International Copyright Secured.

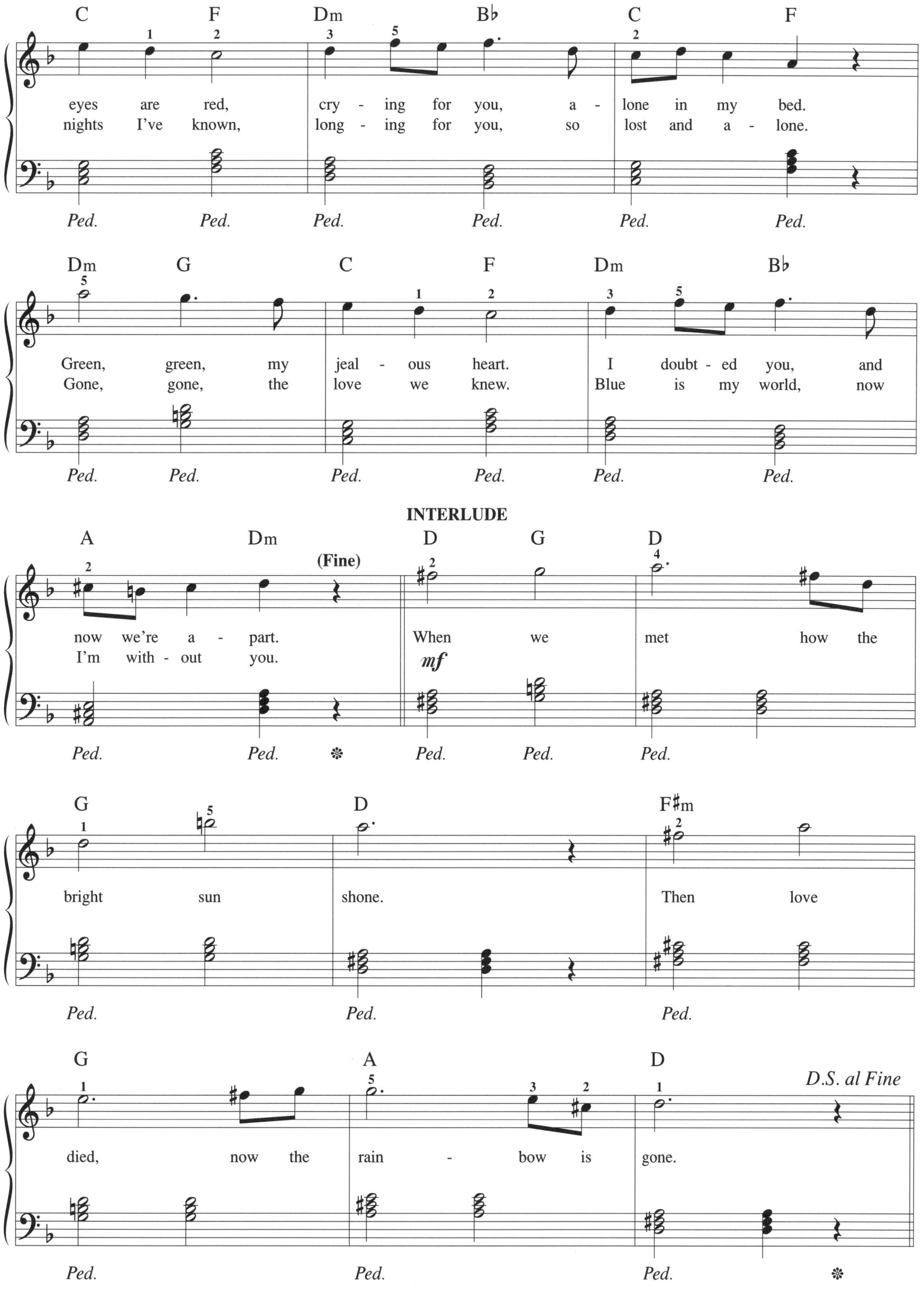
C F Dm B♭ C F
eyes are red, cry - ing for you, a - lone in my bed.
nights I've known, long - ing for you, so lost and a - lone.
Ped. Ped. Ped. Ped. Ped. Ped.
Dm G C F Dm B♭
Green, green, my jeal - ous heart. I doubt - ed you, and
Gone, gone, the love we knew. Blue is my world, now
Ped. Ped. Ped. Ped. Ped. Ped.
INTERLUDE
A Dm D G D
(Fine)
now we're a - part. When we met how the
I'm with - out you.
mf
Ped. Ped. Ped. Ped. Ped.
G D F♯m
bright sun shone. Then love
Ped. Ped. Ped.
G A D
D.S. al Fine
died, now the rain - bow is gone.
Ped. Ped. Ped.

World

Words & Music by Barry Gibb, Robin Gibb & Maurice Gibb

♩ = 126

CHORUS

Now I've found that the world is round, and of course it rains ev'ry day.

BRIDGE

Living tomorrow, where in the world will I

© Copyright 1967 & 1975 Gibb Brothers Music.
All Rights Reserved. International Copyright Secured.

be? To - mor - row, how far am I a - ble to see? Or am I need - ed here?

CHORUS

Now I've found that the world is round, and of course it rains ev - 'ry day.

(rit. 2nd time)

(Fine)

Ticket To Ride

Words & Music by John Lennon & Paul McCartney

39

Collections of great jazz, blues, pop, rock and dance music for intermediate standard piano solo.

Each piece is arranged and fingered in authentic style and includes helpful playing and style notes, fingering and chord symbols.

JUST BLUES
Basin Street Blues, Angel Eyes,
The Lady Sings The Blues
...and many more.
CH61056

JUST JAZZ
Caravan, Fascinating Rhythm,
Lullaby of Birdland
...and many more.
CH61057

JUST LATIN
The Girl From Ipanema,
One Note Samba, Desafinado
...and many more.
CH61217

JUST ROCK
Wonderwall, All Shook Up,
Can't Buy Me Love
...and many more.
CH61218

JUST POP
Unchained Melody, Fernando,
Every Breath You Take, Hey Jude
...and many more.
CH61280

JUST SWING
Honeysuckle Rose,
Sophisticated Lady, Come Fly With Me
...and many more.
CH61281

JUST RAGS
The Entertainer, Maple Leaf Rag,
Black And White Rag
...and many more.
CH61282

Also in this series:
JUST JAZZ for alto saxophone and piano accompaniment
JUST BLUES for alto saxophone and piano accompaniment

Chester Music Limited
Exclusive distributors:
Music Sales Limited, Newmarket Road,
Bury St Edmunds, Suffolk IP33 3YB.